T0021225

Thanks to park ranger Werner Van Hove.

Copyright © 2022 Clavis Publishing Inc., New York

Originally published as *De boswachter* in Belgium and the Netherlands by Clavis Uitgeverij, 2020
English translation from the Dutch by Clavis Publishing Inc., New York

Visit us on the Web at www.clavis-publishing.com.

Park Rangers and What They Do (small size edition) written and illustrated by Liesbet Slegers

ISBN 978-1-60537-775-9

This book was printed in April 2022 at Graspo CZ, a.s., Pod Šternberkem 324, 76302 Zlín, Czech Republic.

First Edition
10 9 8 7 6 5 4 3 2 1

Park Rangers
and What They Do

Liesbet Slegers

Clavis

NEW YORK

management plan

It's nice to take a walk in the forest.
There's a lot to see and hear!
Are there any trees with dead branches
that can fall onto the trail?
Did any rare animals pass by?
The park ranger keeps an eye on it all.
Do you want to come along through the forest,
together with the park ranger?

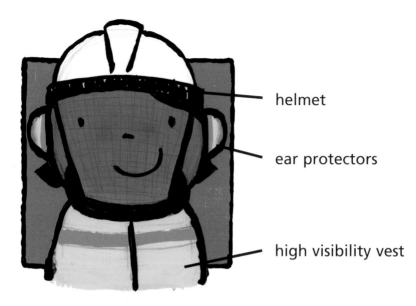

helmet

ear protectors

high visibility vest

The park ranger wears **clothes** in the **colors of the forest:** shades of brown and green. That way, she doesn't stand out between the trees and she doesn't disturb the animals. The park ranger always wears **long pants with pockets** and **sturdy hiking boots** or **rain boots.** That way, her legs and feet are protected from animals that sting. Attached to a **special belt,** she carries her tools. In case of dangerous work, the park ranger wears a **helmet** and **ear protection.** The **safety vest** is used by the park ranger when she works at the edge of the forest.

park ranger's hat

park ranger's clothes

belt with tools

rain boots

warm winter coat

sturdy hiking boots

night camera

Various tools are attached to the belt, such as a **small** and a big **flashlight,** a handy **pocketknife,** and **binoculars.** In **animal and plant guidebooks,** the park ranger can look up rare species. With her **smartphone,** she makes calls and photographs animal tracks. The GPS helps her find her way. The **night camera** shoots footage of animals that pass by at night. In the **management plan,** the park ranger reads what the forest should look like now and in the future. With the **caliper,** she measures the thickness of a tree trunk, with the **altimeter,** she measures the height of a tree. And with the **marking axe,** she puts a stamp on the trees that have to be cut down.

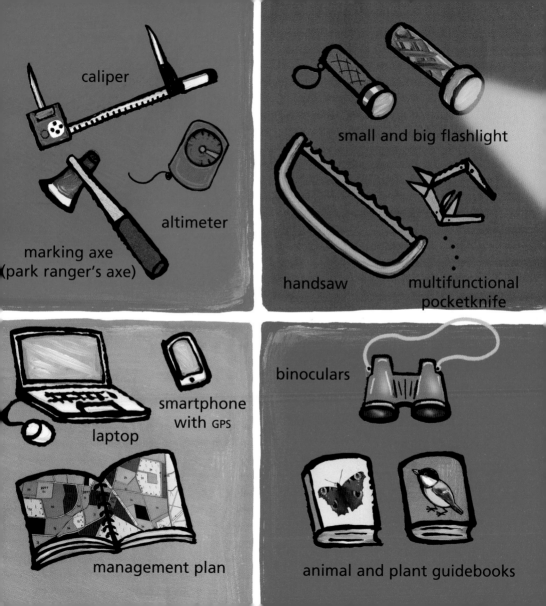

caliper

altimeter

marking axe
(park ranger's axe)

small and big flashlight

handsaw

multifunctional
pocketknife

laptop

smartphone
with GPS

management plan

binoculars

animal and plant guidebooks

Last night, the park ranger was sleeping peacefully. Suddenly, a violent storm broke out with thunder and lightning! The next morning, the park ranger wakes up early, and thinks of her forest. Hopefully, not many trees were blown over last night . . .
She quickly answers a few questions on her laptop and heads out. After that storm, it's going to be a busy day in the forest today!

The park ranger walks her route through the forest.
One big tree fell over and a thick branch was torn off.
The park ranger calls the forestry workers, who are also
already at work in the forest, "Can you saw the tree
into pieces and remove it?" The park ranger passes
on the location of the fallen tree. With her little
handsaw, she clears up the torn off branch herself.

Trees that were cut down are often used to make furniture.

altimeter

The park ranger has taken a good look at her forest management plan. In this place, beautiful oaks have been growing for hundreds of years. This has to stay that way. So, the other tree species growing can't stay here. First, the park ranger measures the trees that have to go. With the caliper, she finds out exactly how thick a tree is. When she measures the height with the altimeter, she knows how much money can be earned by selling the wood of the tree.

Now the park ranger marks the trees that have to go with her marking axe. With the axe side, she chips away some bark, and with the stamp side, she slams a stamp into the bare, soft wood. Then the park ranger puts blue dots on the trees that have to stay with a special spray can. Thanks to the stamps and the dots, the workers can see which trees can be cut down and which can't.

Suddenly, the park ranger hears a birdsong that she
doesn't recognize. Quickly, she grabs her binoculars.
Wow, she hasn't seen that bird species around here
very often yet. Maybe new beetles that this bird likes to
eat are living in the forest. She'll investigate that later.
But first, she walks over to the night camera. It's hanging
in this place because deer often cross the trail here.
Did the camera shoot some footage of deer last night?
Or maybe a wolf, a fox, or a beaver was seen?

Oh no, what happened here? A big pile of trash was dumped. How awful! Who would have done this?
The park ranger notes down what happened: she makes a report, just like the police do, and takes pictures. Maybe someone has seen something? She'll certainly sort it out.

The park ranger arrives at an open area where only grass grows. The grass has been mowed already, but it needs to be even shorter. That's why a farmer from the neighborhood will bring his flock of sheep to graze. But first, the forestry workers install an enclosure, so the sheep won't get lost in the forest later on.

Here comes the farmer with his sheep. Hey, there's a donkey too. The park ranger checks everything thoroughly. Is the enclosure okay? Do the animals feel good here? She thanks the forestry workers for the enclosure. Now the sheep and the donkey can graze calmly. Soon, the grass will be very short and then the animals can go back to the farm.

A nature walk in the forest has been planned for that night. Grown-ups and children walk through the forest in the dark together with the park ranger. If they're very quiet and don't disrupt the animals, they might see a snout of a porcupine or hear the beautiful tawny owl call: hoot! – hoot!

Thank you, park ranger, for taking care of the forest and protecting nature. That way, the forest remains a nice place for the trees, the animals, and of course, also for the people who come to visit!

Does the park ranger do these activities in spring, summer, autumn, or winter?

A hiker has picked many mushrooms. The park ranger says he isn't allowed to do that. The mushrooms are necessary in the forest because they clear up the fallen leaves.

In autumn

It's hot. The park ranger watches and counts the butterflies that are flying over the field. That way, she finds out a lot about the flowers and the plants here. And also whether the field may be getting too dry.

In summer